MW00846850

I FELL FOUR MILES AND LIVED

Missing in Action
World War II

Complete and Unabridged

James Andrew Raley

Jamesgate Press LLC

"I Fell Four Miles and Lived
Missing in Action-World War II"
Complete and Unabridged
James Andrew Raley
The Falling Fortress Series (Third)

Edited by M. A. Raley from the original memoir "War Story,"
also titled "James A. Raley Missing in Action-World War II"

Proofing:
P.G. Sullivan and J.L. Cavender

Cover by
Jamesgate Press and DKDC Design www.dkdcdesign.com

© 2013 Jamesgate Press LLC
All Rights Reserved

ISBN-13: 978-0615904740
ISBN-10: 0615904742

For the US Airmen who died
11 January 1944

"God bless your souls, you brave and immortal
dead."

I FELL FOUR MILES AND LIVED

Preface

During the economic turmoil in the U.S. in the years just before World War II, James Andrew Raley, a farm boy from Kentucky, joined the 1st Armored Cavalry, 13th Regiment, served in Operation Torch in Northern Africa, and later transferred to the Army Air Forces. On his 13th mission, while serving as a tail gunner on a B-17, he survived a midair collision over the Peloponnesus and a subsequent four-mile turbulent descent in the severed tail section into enemy territory. He then reunited with other survivors, who were able to evade the enemy for three months before escaping.

This is the complete and unabridged version of Raley's account, which was written in 1945, a year after it occurred. Raley used two different titles for his memoir: "War Story," and "James A. Raley Missing in Action World War II." A much shortened version of this memoir was published as "I Fell Four Miles and Lived: Missing in Action--World War II (Abridged Version)" by Jamesgate Press in September 2013.

Introduction

On 11 January 1944, I was a member of a B-17 (Flying Fortress) bomber squadron situated near Foggia, Italy. The target for the day was enemy shipping at a port near Athens, Greece. We took off at about 1000 hours. We flew south and east to a point over the Ionian Sea. There we turned and headed east to the target. We were over the Peloponnesus, ascending at about 20,000 feet altitude, when disaster struck. The time was about 40 minutes past noon. Eight aircraft bearing about 70 crewmen were lost; 16 crewmen survived. Greece was enemy-occupied territory at the time. This account was written about one year following.

1. Mission of the Day

I had put on the flying gear -- the electrically heated suit, shoes, the Mae West, the parachute, the speaking device for the interphone system, and headset before leaving the ground, and had made my way to the tail section before we had cleared the ground a hundred feet.

Everything down below looked very pretty. I had made sufficient hops from that region to feel that that section of Italy was as familiar to me as my home town. I was having a happy time of it, watching things in general, keeping the pilot posted on the situation as I saw it, and arguing with the other gunners on the intercom. It was much fun. Finally we headed out to the sea. We kept gaining altitude and Italy grew proportionately smaller.

Soon, I could see the outline of the "boot" we used to study about in school.

We flew out over the Adriatic, gaining altitude rapidly. I could no longer see the waves on the sea, which took on a glassy smoothness that indicated that we were "up." At about 10,000 feet we put on the oxygen mask. After that, the navigator called out the altitude regularly. Everyone "rogered in" to indicate that all was well. The heavens were beautiful. Formations of B-17's were strung for miles to the rear. The sky was clear. The formation perfect. The navigator called back the altitude -- 19,000 feet -- as we kept ascending. I glanced at my watch. It was 1240 hours. All was well. Tiny vapor trails began to form. The beauty of them distracted me. We flew into a cloud bank.

Suddenly there was a great ripping, tearing sensation, and accompanying sound. The tail section shuddered and seemed to stop. The tranquil state just moments earlier became one of unimaginable violence. I was facing to the rear and was thrown astern and down. My face flashed past the guns and slapped against the ship's right ammunition trough. Immediately I began falling and spiraling at a tremendous rate of speed. I was in perfect physical trim and quite strong, so I took steps to extricate myself to take to the parachute. After several minutes of violent, surging effort, I realized that the centrifugal force exerted by the falling, spinning motion of the ship abolished any probability of my ever freeing myself. Abruptly I was faced with death, sudden and inescapable.

I was conscious then of a feeling or sense of futility and resignation that seemed to creep over me. I could visualize the awful mess the crashed plane would make. I could see myself and fellow crewmen smeared over the countryside. I thought of what a horrible corpse I would be - but I did not dwell on that for long. This new emergency called for renewed energy, in a different vein. I suddenly remembered all the prayers Mother had taught me in years gone by. I achieved a very high

state of religious fervor. I recalled a myriad
of things I wished I had not done. My whole
life passed in a panorama of the many little
incidents. Time dragged on maddeningly. I
began to want very much for it to be over and
done. If I was to die, I wanted to die, not to
spend the remainder of my life fretting in an-
ticipation. Finally, there was a great swishing
sound as we crashed through the tops of some
small trees, and as abruptly as the chaos had
begun, it stopped. I lay still, certain in the
knowledge that I was among the deceased.
This thought had not done me any good. The
outer covering of the ship was in shreds. The
barrels of my two guns were bent nearly double. I was shaken. I opened my eyes, and
slowly, very slowly, came to realize that I was
not dead at all. Looking past the guns, I could
see the earth, pebbles, and vegetation. The
ship had come to rest in a dense growth of
shrubs.

I became aware of a cracking sound,
like a rapidly burning fire, and imagined the
ship was on fire. I suddenly became very in-

terested in freeing myself. The inside of the compartment was in disarray. Everything was wrong. Debris was piled high on my back. The left side of the ship was stove in. My right leg was between the ammunition box and seat. It required about all the effort I could manage for me to extricate myself, but at last I was free.

I realized that the ship was sitting on an even keel and what I had thought was a burning fire was actually the snapping of twigs as the plane settled into its new resting place. I knew that escape via the hatch intended for that purpose would be impossible, as it was directly on the ground, so I would have to use the bulkhead passage into the waist section. I kept thinking of my fellow crewmen, the others in the plane, wondering if they too were alive and if I would be able to assist them. I made a mental bet that the bulkhead door would be jammed and that I would not be able to open it, but I was mistaken. The bulkhead door worked perfectly. When it swung open, the heaps of wreckage I had expected to see were not there at all. Instead, all I could see was geography – trees on the hillside – in quantity. Astonished, I stepped out of the tail section. I glanced at the watch which was still ticking merrily. It was 1330 -- thirty minutes since the last time I had checked. I looked skyward. There were lots of clouds. Too bad, I thought. Otherwise, we would be on the way back.

I surveyed the wreckage. The tail section was in sad shape. The bottom was in shreds. The stabilizers were broken and hanging in pieces. Small particles of metal, the size of a coin, tiny lengths of fuel line, and electrical wiring were scattered thickly about. I stared at that part of the tail compartment where it had broken away from the rest of the ship. It had sheared off just forward of the bulkhead, the partition that separates the waist and the tail sections. The break was amazingly even. It was as though the plane had been opened by a large can opener.

Frequently since then, I have debated with myself and others as to how I happened to be there. By rumor, theory, speculation, and official report, I have concluded that it was something like this.

For that mission we had turned out four groups. The 2nd Bombardment Group led, and after them came our group, the 301st. Practically everything had gone according to the big plan until a few minutes before the lead group was over the target. It seems that two ships from that group, for reasons of mechanical failure, turned back and were returning to their base in Italy when they too entered the cloud bank on the same altitude as our formation. The planes must have met head on. When they collided, there was great violence. The air was filled with debris, the sounds of great explosions, and planes rent asunder. We had apparently cleared the cloud bank by this time, as I had seen several B-17's on fire and in varying stages of destruction.

It was not long before I became interested in my own physical condition. Sitting there, I realized that I kept wanting to ease my body down to a position where I could recline – to rest my back and shoulders against the boulder. Breathing was a great effort. Inhaling was in little puffs only. Several days passed before a deep breath was possible. It occurred to me that I should be suffering from shock. I wondered what the result would be.

For some reason I decided to make my way down the mountainside. With considerable effort, I got to my feet and moved back to the ship where I gathered up a pair of GI shoes and electrically heated gauntlets, RAF type. I remember feeling highly delinquent when I decided to leave the many other items of equipment behind. I tied the shoelaces together, put on the gloves, noted that I had the escape kit in my pocket, and started the long descent down the northern slope of Mount Oros.

The going was quite steep and was made worse by the uneven terrain. I managed to half-climb, half fall from tree to tree down the almost perpendicular mountainside for possibly a hundred yards, when I came upon a trail that bore marks of recent use. Here, I figured, was the place best suited for rescue. Somebody was sure to come by and see me; then my worries would be over. I sat down on another boulder, and before long found myself again in a reclining position. Eventually I was lying all the way across the trail. After much effort, I again was on my feet and hobbling toward a small stream. The right knee was almost completely useless by then.

Upon reaching the stream, I found that I wasn't capable of lowering myself to it to drink. In addition to the knee, the back, chest and shoulders were out of commission. At last, I threw myself to the ground and drank as best I could. This, I found, was highly unsatisfactory. Having quenched my thirst, I came to a sitting position and was able to maneuver myself back to the original spot without getting to my feet.

As I lay there, the rain beating into my face, I kept thinking and turning over in my mind what had happened, and wondering what I was to do. I was in the center of a fold or recess in the mountainside. The trail wound around and disappeared beyond the shoulders of the recess. The area was heavily wooded. Looking down, a matter of miles, into the valley below, I could see a number of houses and one place that had the appearance of a fortress -- walls, parapets and all. I wished that I were down there.

Suddenly something moved over at the right. I looked closely and saw a man -- small, skinny, ragged, and bareheaded. He was peeping around the corner, or turn in the trail, and through the trees and branches. I yelled, "Hey, come here -- please" and was surprised at the weakness of my voice.

The sightseer disappeared. I figured he would be back and congratulated myself for choosing such a likely spot to hit the ground. Pretty soon the same thing happened again -- this time to the left. Whoever the visitor was he had some military connection apparently, as he was wearing an olive drab overcoat with brass buttons. I wondered if he were friend or foe -- then reminded myself that this was no time to quibble. At that moment I would have relished being in a German hospital.

Odd thoughts flitted through my mind as I lay on the ground. I mentally followed the bombers to the target and back to the base -- checking the time and imagining they would be at a certain point by now. I thought now and again of the old folks back home. By subtracting seven hours from local time, I could imagine what they were doing.

At that point, two more visitors appeared. These two were brave. They were middle-aged women and came from the left side. They didn't bother to stop and peep as

the others did. In fact, they didn't bother to
stop -- period. They were gossiping animat-
edly. When they came to me, they stepped
over my prostrate body and kept on walking,
never checking the stride. I called after them,
suggesting that they stop, but they never both-
ered to look back.

A few minutes later and another lady
passed by. She took time out for word of
greeting and then went merrily on her way.
During the next two hours, a dozen or more
people passed along the trail. Some of them
stopped, some did not. All of them had to
step over me to pass. At about 1700 hours,
daylight began to rapidly diminish, and I rea-
soned that I should try to find a better place to
spend the night. I scrambled haltingly to my
feet and began moving away to the left. I
rounded the turn in the trail. I had proceeded
a short way when I found that the trail turned
sharply to the left again and led up the mountainside, instead of along the relatively level
course. I realized that my travels for that day

were drawing to a close. I climbed upward for a few feet and fell exhausted.

It was nearly dark by then. A short distance from the trail I could see a tree with dense foliage, which I decided would afford an ideal shelter for the night. I moved over to the tree and found the earth under the branches quite dry. I stretched out on the ground and became reasonably comfortable, making a pillow of the shoes and gloves and removing the escape kit from my hip pocket. The clothing I was wearing was not exactly suited for the business I was engaged in, although it was fine for flying. I wore two suits of GI coveralls, with an electrically heated flying suit in between. The inner suit protected me from broken and shorted wires, while the outer one protected the heated suit from snags and soil. The heated shoes were worthless, except for flying, so if I planned at any time while in Greece to do any walking, I had best hang onto the GI shoes. I lay there staring up at the branches overhead, wondering when I could reasonably expect to get back to Italy. I thought about opening the escape kit and tearing into some of the concentrated food, but decided to wait until the next day.

Suddenly, I heard voices shouting in the distance. This was heartening. The voices seemed far away. I decided against wasting my strength unnecessarily, in the hope that they would come nearer. A minute or so later they called again. This time they were closer. They were coming up from the valley I had seen in the afternoon. When they had reached a point in the vicinity of the spot where I had spent the afternoon holding up traffic, I began to try to attract their attention. I tried to whistle, but somehow I made no sound. I tried again and again, with the same result. I called to them, but my voice was strong enough to carry only a few feet. Curses! What was I going to do? I had wandered away from the trail to bed down under the tree. Now I was too weak to make myself heard or to move back to the trail to intercept the searchers -- whoever they were. Pretty soon I could see them in the faint light moving up the trail that led past the tree that was serving as my shelter. They were only a few feet away and plainly visible. I called to them in the loudest voice I could manage. They heard me.

2. A Stay at the Monastery

There were about five or six of them. Shepherds. Small, skinny, unshaven, poorly dressed. However, each earned my eternal gratitude during the next three and a half hours. They helped me down the mountainside. Most of the time, the trail was wide enough for only one man. It was strewn with boulders and was very steep. Two of them would assist me along, one on either side, my arms about their shoulders. Every fifteen or twenty minutes, they would change about. I can imagine what a burden I must have been, as I outweighed any one of them by at least fifty pounds.

As we approached the village, after reaching the valley, I could see two young men walking towards me. One of them embraced me, kissed me on both cheeks and said, "My friend." This came to me as a surprise. I remarked that he could speak English -- which he could, two words of it.

At the village I was given a slug of "ouzo," a Greek ambrosia, a kind of whitish, almost clear fluid similar to stimulant popular in my native Kentucky. I was placed on a donkey and taken for a canter along the floor of the valley. That was my first ride on mule back in Greece, but certainly not my last. Back in Kentucky, I had considered myself quite the horseman, but now, the hungry little donkey with the wooden packsaddle arrangement and no stirrups took lots of getting used to.

After about half an hour of hanging on for dear life as we bounced along up and down sharp little hills, forded flooded streams, and rushed under low hanging branches, we started up a long and rather steep incline. As we neared the top I could see outlined against the sky a walled in compound and suddenly realized that this was the fortress-like building I had seen during the afternoon.

The trail led around two sides of the stone wall to a point where there was a huge double door or gate constructed of heavy timbers, about 20 feet by 20 feet in dimension. The man who was leading the donkey approached the door and banged several times with the heavy knocker. Pretty soon there was the sound of footsteps on the cobblestones. Inside the stockade, I heard the rasping of the latch being thrown, and, shortly, the loud creaking of one of the doors swinging on its rusty hinges.

A small, black-clothed figure stepped through the opening and conversed with the mule driver. I gathered that the newcomer was a man also, though he wore a flowing, dress-like garment. The two of them helped me down from the mule and inside the stockade. We paused long enough for the host to close the gate and then proceeded along the cobblestoned courtyard to a flight of steps. Then we continued down a long veranda to a door that was being held open by another local. We entered a room about 30 feet square, jammed full of people. Among these were four Americans -- a navigator, two radio operators, and a photographer. We all began jabbering at the same time, telling each other how it happened. Neil Daley, the navigator, listened to my story and remarked that my mode of descent was incredible. Some of the ladies in the gathering made a pallet of blankets beside the open fireplace and others assisted me in lying down.

None of the Greeks present could speak English, so we Americans confined our remarks to each other. I gathered that we were at a monastery that was being held together by a couple of Eastern Orthodox Priests and four or five Nuns who had been driven out of their homes at Pyrgos by the Germans; that we were in the northern part of the Peloponnesian Peninsula, south and east of the port city of Patras; and that a doctor was on his way to take care of us. Much of this news was communicated by a Greek who spoke a bit of French to an American who understood a bit of French -- both were illiterate in the language.

The navigator, Daley, was in a bad way. He was lying on a makeshift bed, breathing more quickly than I was, and apparently suffering severely. He mentioned that he had made his descent in a half parachute and had been bounced around considerably when he landed. Eventually the doctor arrived. He had with him a Greek called John, who had lived in the USA for some time and spoke a pretty good grade of English. John the Interpreter was about all the doctor brought. He had no medical supplies or instruments to speak of. He managed to give Daley, the navigator, a hypodermic and to bandage some of his abrasions. He inspected various parts of my body and remarked to the interpreter, who passed the remark on to me, "There's nothing wrong with you." To this I responded, "He's crazy as hell." Fortunately, the doctor didn't understand English. He prescribed hot compresses for the knee and calf of my right leg. That is all the medical attention I ever received. The doctor did everything possible to comfort us. During our stay at the monastery he visited us four times. He walked six hours each way to do so.

On the first day we were there, the able-bodied Americans, along with many natives, buried all the bodies they could find. The priests assisted and prayed over the graves, many of which were unidentified.

There was a constant stream of visitors. They came from miles around. They would burst into the room, shake our hands, stand and stare for a while, chat with the other natives, shake our hands again, smile, and leave. Without exception, they were friendly, hospitable, poorly clothed, and undernourished. They would bring gifts of food, which they could ill afford. Daley and I were the only patients. Two of the women volunteered to be our nurses. They were present for nearly one week, 24 hours a day. After the first night at the monastery, our misused bodies became very sensitive. Even the slightest movement was painful. When either of us stirred, a nurse was on hand to help us shift to a more comfortable position and rearrange our covers.

The second night was a busy one. A band of partisans from the ELAS -- the Greek Peoples Liberation Army, a resistance group -- came charging into the monastery. They hogged the fire and made a lot of noise, and kept the room cold with their coming and going. A wild-eyed citizen named Helmas considered himself to be the leader. He looked like a portable arsenal. He G-2ed us regarding possible supplies of arms and ammunition. The next day he left, taking the others with him. A couple of weeks later he did the rope dance for the Germans in Patras.

By the third day, our numbers increased by one -- a gunner. He came in just in time to join the two radio operators and the partisans as they were leaving. That left Daley, Raley (me), and the photographer.

A day or so later, a British Army Captain joined us. He hailed from Eire and was O'Donnell by name, which we soon shortened to OD. He asked haughtily if we wished to see his credentials. I did not and told him that there was nothing I could do about it if he wanted to be unpleasant, but that it made me very happy to hear him talk.

When the partisans departed, they left behind Martin, an English speaking Greek, who had somehow been in some of the best jails in the United States. In fact, Martin's bouts with the law in the States became so frequent that he was finally deported. Our good friend, OD, the British Captain, brought many useful items -- soap, towels, toothbrushes, and toothpaste -- but no razors. When OD took his leave, he left a gold sovereign with Martin, our English speaking self-appointed Greek protector. A sovereign was a British coin worth about $8.00 in America, but worth a man's life at that time in Greece.

Martin the Greek was an operator. I could never understand why he had spent so much time in jail. He undertook to supply us with food and was a sensation. Inflation had struck the Greeks a severe blow. Their currency, the draxma, which was once worth about twenty cents a unit, was deflated to a point where an egg cost a hundred thousand draxmai. This would have been equal to twenty-thousand US dollars. As I said, Martin was an economist. He would bargain for an egg, a bit of fruit, or a loaf of bread, agree on a price, and place the article securely in his gunnysack. He would then very generously offer the gold sovereign as payment. There wasn't enough currency in that part of Greece to make change, so Martin would agree to pay the man as soon as he was able to break the coin down into currency. We lived pretty well for those few days.

3. Moving On

Before leaving, OD had agreed to send a messenger at the end of the second week who would arrange to move us to the central British headquarters at the village of Mikalekah (phonetic) -- if we thought we were equal to the trip, that is. The British in Greece were with an intelligence movement similar to our OSS. He pointed out that it was seven rough hours, but that there was a village in between where we could rest and refresh ourselves.

Shortly before the time came to leave, our good doctor called on us. Daley gave him a sovereign from his escape kit, over much protesting. The ladies who had nursed us had left after the first week. We gave them a parachute. We also gave a parachute to the Mother Superior of the nuns. She was an enlightened and educated individual. She used to single out the various points of interest in Greece to us on the maps from our escape kits. Martin would interpret what she said, adding much to her narrative.

When Martin arrived, he wore so little clothing, he was practically nude. He would surely have frozen to death had it not been for the armament he carried about himself -- a cartridge belt over each shoulder and a grenade belt about his waist. He carried an Italian carbine, which he said was worthless. He wore no hat or shoes. His only clothing consisted of a sweater and trousers, which were in the last stages of repair. We gave him a flying helmet with pieces cut away for ear phones, a blue heated suit with no button on the back side, and a pair of heated shoes. Seeing him in that get up gave us many laughs.

When the messenger arrived from headquarters we were ready to go. As we were leaving, the nuns wept and the men wrung our hands in friendship. We tried to express our gratitude to them through the in-

terpreter. We then made the jaunt on mule
back -- it was Daley's first try. O'Donnell did
not exaggerate when he said the going would
be rough.

We departed the monastery on Sunday,
23 January, in the early morning. It was well
into the night when we arrived at Mikalekah.
We arrived, both completely exhausted. Here,
we lived in the mayor's house. He had a love-
ly wife and three of the finest children I saw
in Greece. We could never understand how
his children were so husky, when all the other
children seemed half starved. During the oc-
cupation of Greece at this time, infant mortali-
ty reached almost 100%.

The mayor's house, like most of those I
saw, was a two story affair. The live stock
lived down stairs. The upstairs contained two
large rooms with a vestibule in between. The
outside door opened into the vestibule. The
family lived in the kitchen, where there was a
fireplace and a chimney. There was no provi-
sion for heating the room we occupied. I was

bedridden and never ventured from the room more than once or twice during the three weeks we stayed there. The only means I had for keeping the near-zero temperatures out was to call for more blankets. Elaine, who, at seven, was the older of the two girls, used to bring my meals to me. In the evenings she would take the lamp and tray away, and on leaving the room would say, "Goot. Night. Jeem." and I would tell her good night in Greek.

Sometimes during the day the children would play in the room. They would gather around the bed and sing songs. They were colossal on a Greek version of "The Wood-pecker's Song." I tried to teach them "Tra, Rah, Rah, Boom-de-Yea," but they stalled out on the R's. I tried, with even less success, to teach them "Deep in the Heart of Texas." However, they mastered "Row, Row, Row Your Boat" in no time at all.

Mikalekah was a very busy place. There were several Britons on hand, commis-

sioned and otherwise. The town was strategi-
cally situated, being a relatively short distance
from Patras, the center of much German activity, and in the center of other Allied estab-
lishments. Greek runners in British uniform
were coming and going at all hours. Now and
then, the Nazis would make a demonstration
and put the natives on edge. Fortunately, they
never became sufficiently hostile while we
were there to cause us a great deal of anxiety.

About the first of February, an odd situation arose. A Messerschmitt ME-210 had
been buzzing during the afternoon. It was
generally thought that the pilot was trying to
spot the radio. That was remedied by going
off the air and spending the afternoon in light
conversation. Towards dusk, a navigator (not
Daley) who had "assumed" command of the
AAF personnel in that part of Greece, burst
into the room, wild-eyed, jabbering something
about a "Hun scare." Hun scare was British
for an enemy attack. He told me to be brave
and not to worry, as he would take care of me.
He said further that if they came too close,

we'd leave town, at least temporarily. I assured him that I wouldn't wander off, as I couldn't walk anyway, whereupon he departed as rapidly as he had come.

Dinner was served as usual, and by the time I had finished and Elaine had removed the dishes and lamp, the room was quite dark. I settled myself in bed for a long night. It was about 1830 hours. I had dozed during the afternoon, so the likelihood of falling asleep right away was slight. I lay there staring at where the ceiling should have been, thinking about this and that, wondering when I'd be well again, if ever. I also wondered whether we would get out of Greece any time soon. I concocted a few new ways of getting out, though none of which applied to me, as I was unable to walk. My thoughts turned to the folks in Kentucky. It would have been about noon there. I was wondering how they had reacted to the sudden lull in my letter writing, when I heard the roar of aircraft engines.

Almost immediately there were the sounds of excited male Greek voices outside my window. These were joined by a great multitude of other voices, male and female, Greek and English. There were desperate shouts and screams, curses, frantic footsteps chasing about on the icy snow and cobble-stones. Doors were slammed, children screeched, guns were fired. There was the braying of donkeys, the clip clop of trotting hooves, the barking and yapping of dogs -- a wild pandemonium of sounds -- all of which abruptly ceased, less than five minutes after they had begun. Absolute quiet prevailed. As I lay there, practically unable to move. I could hear my watch ticking. I asked myself, "Is this a Hun scare, have they left without me?"

Obviously they had, for during the next hour and a half no sound was forthcoming, from any direction. I busied myself by think-ing horrible thoughts. I estimated that the en-emy would arrive somewhere between one and two hours after the alarm. I set to won-dering what I was to do. That I answered quickly -- nothing. I speculated upon what was to happen to me. Would they set fire to the house without first searching it? Would some German come into the room and shoot me? I had the questionable satisfaction of knowing that I would find out without having to wait very long. This was as miserable a position as I have ever been in.

The waiting had been in progress for the better part of two hours. By that time I had grown tired of "sweating" and was trying to think of something pleasant, when in the distance I heard the thumping of many footsteps. The footsteps drew nearer. I could hear male voices. The intruders stopped just outside the window. There was a brief period of conversation. I rose up in bed and tried to open the wooden shutter that served the dual function of window and blackout curtain. It was stuck -- and so was I. I heard footsteps scurrying up the stairs outside. The outer door was thrown open, and almost immediately, so was the door to my room. I was staring in that direction, but could see nothing.

A voice called out, "Hey Jim." It was Jack Murray, a gunner from the 301st Bombardment Group. He set to telling me about how an Allied plane had flown over and dropped a quantity of supplies some distance away and how all and sundry had turned out to gather them up and bring them to the local storage point. He wound up by saying that I should have been along. I told him I wished very much that I could have been.

4. The Trek to the South

On the 14th of February we took leave of our good friends in Mikalekah and began the trek to the South, with the thought of making our escape from Greece uppermost in our minds. The snow was deep that day and the terrain uncertain. Several in the party were mounted on a motley array of donkeys; however, I rode a horse. He was perhaps 16 hands high and very skinny. He was a demon for speed when we were going downhill, but his master would have to get behind and shove him when we were going upgrade.

Shortly before we began our trek southward, there was some discussion among the British as to who would go and who would not. Neil Daley and I were selected to remain behind. I was not aware of that until much later. I have never learned who made the trip possible for me. When asked if I were able to make the trip, I insisted that I was the man most likely to succeed. That first day proved that I was mistaken. The journey took the better part of two weeks. The ultimate destination was the town of Zacharo, which was south of Pyrgos and near the Ionian Sea. The distance by air was possibly fifty miles, probably less. There is no way of knowing, but I dare say we traveled a hundred and fifty miles via the overland route. One of the most satisfying experiences I have ever known was reaching the end of the line. To anyone who hasn't experienced something closely related to it, any description of the tribulations we found along the way will be a waste of effort.

Erick, a native Greek who had been educated at Oxford and given a spot commission as subaltern in the British Army, was designated as kingpin of the party. He was charged with seeing us safely out of the country. He was high-handed, loud mouthed, and obnoxious, but he did his job pretty well.

Our party grew in numbers. Early in the season there were 16 Americans, Erick the Greek, and the owners of the donkeys. Each day we used different animals -- the owners returned to their homes at the end of the day. Pretty soon we gathered up three or four members of the erstwhile occupational troops of the Italian Army. They were a sad lot. Their best defense was the fact that they were with the British and Americans. The Greeks were outspoken in their dislike for them. Later, we came upon other British, one of whom was a flyer who had been shot down, more Italians, Greeks, Cretans, Cypriots, deserters from the German Army (French, Czech, and Austrian nationals), a Russian, and Herbie Myers.

Herbie was a great guy with a story to tell. He was in his early twenties, tall, blonde, and handsome. His home and family were in Union City, New Jersey, but not Herbie, no. Instead, he said, he had set out some years before to circumnavigate the globe. He went via San Francisco, Japan, China, Russia, and then to Berlin. In Berlin, the authorities placed the clamp on him and slapped him into service in the once great Wehrmacht. He had a large time of it -- in and out of the guardhouse, on to the Russian front, and then Berlin, until he was finally sent to Greece where he went "over the hill" and joined up with us.

In the last days of our tour, our party numbered 40-odd, and was as unimpressive a crew as you will ever see. All wore cast-off and worn out uniforms of the American, British, Italian, German, and Greek armies. Many had no shoes, but wrapped their feet in rags. Most were hatless and needed haircuts and a shave. Many were suffering from old injuries of skin rashes and huge, ugly, running sores. Nobody was happy. I could think of many places I would have preferred to have been.

The first day was not the hardest. We moved out at about 0800 and traveled steadily until noon, at which time we halted in a village for lunch. I was very pleased to get off the steed and recline on a pallet near a fire.

Erick, the Greek, had arranged for the accommodations by forging ahead of the party and arriving at the village some time before us. Erick was oddly dressed. He wore a British uniform -- of sorts. He had on field shoes, heavy socks, khaki shorts, battle jacket, and no head gear. Seeing him plow through deep snow drifts in near zero temperatures would cause one to wonder.

Late in the afternoon of the first day, we halted for a moment at a village. I was helped down from the tall horse. My feet were cold and I was, along with the others, uncomfortable. There was a lot of loud talk and gesticulating among the Greeks. It seemed that we were supposed to reach another village beyond a certain mountain range before we were to call it a day. The day, however, was at an end and night was upon us. Ahead was a mountain towering not less than 2,500 feet above us. Outlined dimly against the sky was a depression or notch, through which we were to pass. Snow was drifted along the unbroken trail, which no one had traveled since the last snow had fallen. I was in favor of spending the night where we were, but that was not in keeping with the big plan, so we moved on again.

Those on foot moved ahead rapidly, and soon were tiny, dark figures outlined against the snow. The terrain was as rugged as elsewhere, except that the trail led steadily uphill most of the time instead of the uphill, downhill routine we had become accustomed to. Dusk faded into night, but with the snow and grey clouds, it was never completely dark.

As we ascended the mountain side, the snow became deeper. About half way up my large steed, Man O'War as we called him, came to a slow, grinding halt and refused to go further. We coaxed him, but he apparently had had enough. At that point I made a foolish move. I dismounted, hitched the nag onto the donkey ahead that had been vacated by Daley, took hold of the horse's tail, and set off up the mountain side. Before long, Man O'War broke his tow line and made off back in the general direction from which we had come. I detached myself from him and discovered that I had expended all the strength I had. I climbed aboard the donkey and was soon atop the mountain. It was then that I realized that I was in for a session of grief. Up to that point it hadn't occurred to me that the ascent was the better part of mountain climbing.

For some reason it seemed much darker going down the mountain, although the snow was just as deep. Except for places where the trail breakers had removed the snow down to the earth, the trail was invisible. The little donkey, which had been so willing up to this point, wanted no part of the descent.

Far in the distance were lights. Someone had said that that was our destination. The donkey was wearing the usual wooden

packsaddle arrangement, which was without
upholstery and stirrups. After some coaxing,
the donkey set off down the incline. It is hard
to imagine a more perilous undertaking. As I
have said, the trail was invisible -- if there
were a trail. The terrain was exceedingly
rugged. It was possible, if one lost his footing, to soar a considerable distance before
striking a ledge sufficiently wide to break the
fall. The mount proceeded slowly, picking his
way, exercising all caution. His back was in
an almost vertical position -- nose down.
Staying aboard was an achievement. My bum
leg and shoulders were working overtime. I
placed my hands against the front of the sad-
dle to avoid somersaulting over the donkey's
head. That went on for an hour or so. Several
times I wanted to abandon the whole project.
At last, it came to an end when we reached
the village.

We were in the village, the name of
which I don't recall, but which was situated
only a short ways from the village of Kalavryta. The village Kalavryta had been destroyed,

along with its population, by the enemy just before the time of our arrival in Greece. In retribution for the partisans capturing and killing 81 German soldiers, the Germans ordered all the males from the village aged 14 years and older into a field and machine-gunned them. Of around 700 men, only about a dozen survived.

We converged on the local town hall, which was dimly lit by the conventional olive oil lamp. Many people were present. Someone helped me down from my trusty mount and stood by while I leaned heavily on his shoulder. Erick quickly arranged for housing. My host-to-be was present, and because his house being some distance away, it was decided that I should ride the donkey to it. Greeks, generally, are quick to take action when a course has been decided upon. The instant it was ruled that I was to remount, four or five of the townspeople nearest me laid hold and tossed me aboard. One man grasped me about the chest and squeezed mightily on the way up. That did it. All my tribulations were forgotten for the moment. I passed out cold. I could not have been out long, as I was standing beside the mule when I woke up. I asked the men to be a little more gentle the next time. Although there wasn't an English speaker in the crowd, it worked. I went to bed without supper that night, but had no trouble going to sleep.

Next day it rained. I was wearing a British Army great coat, which was pretty well saturated by noon. There were no mountains that day, but the trail was especially rough. As I recall, we had no lunch, the plan being to reach the stopping point in the early afternoon.

By about 1400 hours, I was thoroughly soaked and chilled. A couple of times we became lost. Once, while fording a small stream, the donkey lost his footing and I got even wetter. We were all in low spirits. Finally, just before nightfall, we came to the top of a ridge. In the distance was the goal for the day. Everyone took off, each on his own.

The riders were the last to arrive. As we
passed through the miserable little village,
some member of the party poked his head out
of a door and yelled that I was to "go that
way," indicating the house in which I was to
spend the night.

The driver helped me down and immediately took his leave. I made my way up the
steep incline to the house on hands and knees.
Don Bennett of Alma, Nebraska, rushed out
and assisted me into the house. I was taken to
the kitchen. The house was the usual two
room and vestibule arrangement. A mighty
fire was going. Our hostess quickly laid a pallet alongside the fireplace. I removed the
greatcoat, cap, gloves, and shoes. Don assisted me to lie down. Then and there, for the
only time in my recollection, I gave way to
tears. I wept bitterly for several minutes. I
was very near to despair. I don't think anyone
present knew of my weeping, as I had faced
towards the wall and was making a real effort
to conceal it.

5. Dinner with Teddy

The next morning we again departed at day break. Shortly after we left, Erick pointed out a spot possibly four miles distant, saying that was our destination. Sure enough, just at night fall, we arrived at the village he had indicated, after nine or ten hours of heart breaking travel over some of the worst trails imaginable.

Each night we would impose upon some good Greek's hospitality. Always, we would split up, so no more than one or two of us would be at any one house. There was a pack animal in the caravan that was loaded with British Army field rations that were used to augment the local hand out. Frequently, the field rations were not distributed to the house in which we were staying. When that happened, we were in for a lean stay. Towards the end of the trek, about Thursday, the extra rations were used up, and we, therefore, were on our own.

On Friday, we stopped at a village school house. Theodore Everigitis – Teddy – was the mayor. He was a gentleman of sixty-odd who had spent considerable time in America. He adopted me. We proceeded down the hillside to his home, which seemed to be about the most substantial building in the village. Once inside the house, I climbed into Teddy's bed, a makeshift arrangement consisting of two saw horses, some boards and half a dozen blankets. Teddy sat on the floor by the fireside with his back against the wall, and began to tell me his troubles. I sympathized with him and cussed the invader. I was especially moved by his story of how the enemy, on a foraging trip a couple of months ago, had made off with everything in the house in the way of food, blankets, and household goods, and how his ailing wife, bedfast at the time, had died shortly thereafter.

While we were chatting, his grandson, a lad of six or seven, dashed in jubilantly with a dead bird about the size and color of a canary. Teddy explained that the boy had trapped the bird. I congratulated him. Forthwith, the lad ran out of the room and to his mother, telling her what had happened. The host and I returned to our discussion and before long the young lady came into the room and placed a skillet over the fire and set to cooking something. Being busy with the conversation, I was not aware of what she was doing. Quicker than it takes to tell it, she had left the room with the skillet and reappeared with a tray, a glass of water, a glass of wine, a slice of bread, silver cutlery, a napkin, and a large plate, containing three small pieces of meat. Teddy said that this was to be my supper and for me to dig in, so I did.

The food was delicious. The meat was very good -- crisp and crunchy -- and not nearly enough. I polished off the meal in a hurry, and when I'd finished, I told the host how I had enjoyed it. I asked him what kind of meat I had eaten, mentioning the crunchy effect. He said that I had just eaten the bird the lad had trapped, and this crunchy business I spoke of must have been his bones. That was the only time I ever had canary for dinner. It was better than the stewed grass I'd had the night before.

The next say, Saturday, 19 February, was a rough day. It was the kid brother's birthday -- the day he turned eighteen. As I plodded along, I wondered what he was doing and whether he would register for the draft that day. I learned later he had.

Early in the day we had to ford a formidable stream. It was flooded, icy, and about a hundred yards wide. Nearly everyone else had reached the stream by the time I got there. They had organized a ferrying system that was a sight to behold. Two Greek mule drivers had removed their trousers and were shuttling their donkeys back and forth, hauling two passengers on each mule. This was considered to be very funny by everyone present. There was much shouting and laughter. My steed for the day was a lanky, hungry looking mule that did not have his heart in his work. When we started across the river he headed down stream. Soon we were in deep water, where he lost his footing and I again became very wet.

The weather was fair in the early morning except for dense and threatening clouds. Towards noon, rain began to fall. It increased to a downpour. By that time we were moving into higher ground. As the altitude increased, the temperature dropped. By mid-afternoon the rain had turned into sleet. It fell harder than I have ever seen. At one point, it was so rough the mule balked and turned back, facing downwind. Ice piled up on me and the animal until we looked like an ice carving. During that period I entertained many unhappy thoughts.

We arrived in the town of Andritsaina at about 1630 hours. Before long, I was situated in an apartment house with good friend and fellow sufferer, Sid Sherrie, from Rochester, NY. Sid was plagued by a severe skin rash. The doctors in Greece who had seen him did not have medication to treat him. It was sometime later, after less than a week in the 26th General Hospital in Bari, Italy, that he became well again.

We moved on to the town of Garditsa on Monday, 21 February. Not long after our arrival, after we'd had a day or two to rest up, I found that I seemed a bit stronger. We came to know our Greek benefactors much better. Several of us lived in a vacant house that belonged to a local named Jim. He had lived in the States for several years and was a perfect host. His house was next door. He had built the house we occupied for his daughter, who, it seemed, was contemplating matrimony -- a fact that was unknown to any potential groom. She was quite attractive, except that she wore no shoes and had large feet.

Jim was an odd character. He had a trunk full of money, which he kept in our house. We tried to engage him in a crap game. He was eager to exchange his currency for green backs, of which there were a few in the party. We were equally anxious to do business with him when there was something to buy. The British had instructed us not to engage in this sort of thing, but a bite to eat is a bite to eat. We were able to buy fruit, eggs, nuts, and sometimes a loaf of bread.

There was much political activity while we were there. Jim was a candidate for mayor. When we learned of this, we all set out, hammer and tong, to get him elected. Our efforts may have been responsible for his crushing defeat. Towards the end of the campaign, he would come to us, wearing a harried expression, and beg us to stop electioneering. He was finally appointed judge instead.

The villagers were very friendly. Several evenings they threw parties for us that were great fun. Once there was a masquerade party where many of the young men wore the old issue army uniform -- the type with short skirt, long white stockings, and red fez. They would sing songs and dance, and we, in turn, would sing songs. Our singing was not as good quality as theirs. We would sing the "Army Air Corps Song" or "She'll Be Coming 'Round The Mountain," but we never seemed to be using the same words.

We headed south again on the first day of March. A short distance from the starting point, as we reached the summit of a rather high mountain, the guide, a Captain Frazier of the British Army, an archeologist, indicated the mountain nearest us and to the left, which was covered with stones, boulders, and what appeared to be the remains of several ancient stone buildings. He remarked, "That's Olympia."

6. Waiting, Waiting, Waiting . . .

Our travels ended on March 4th. We
had spent the night in a town, the name of
which I don't recall. We arose early the following morning and set off again on fresh and
spirited donkeys. The mountainous country
to the North had been very cold, but on this
historic morning as we left the little village,
the air seemed full of promise. The sky was
clear, the ground was only slightly frozen, and
the party was in festive spirits. The guide had
told us that we would arrive at our destination
by noon. The animals were in unusually good
condition and as lively as we were. The men
on foot rushed ahead, gaining considerable
distance over the pack train and the invalids.
The trail led up and up, rather gradually and
for the most part, was very smooth.

When we came upon an abrupt and
steep incline, the donkeys took it in their

stride. In no time, we reached the summit.
Before us lay as pretty a valley as I have ever
seen. It extended for miles and was filled
with tall, slender cypress, as erect as candles;
citrus groves; and picturesque villages all over
the place. The big feature though was the
backdrop. Beyond all this and as far as one
could see, was the Ionian Sea. We paused
there on top of the divide for a breather and to
take in some of the beauty that we had been
missing in the past. I vividly recall the emo-
tions I experienced as I looked down all
around me and out to the sea. I let myself
dwell upon some of the possibilities it held.
With a boat, we could get back to Italy and
civilization, friends, medical attention, food, a
bath, and a change of clothes. I could rid myself of my lice, regain my health and strength,
and get ahead with the war. It never occurred
to me that I might go home.

Soon we moved on again, and as we
did, many changes were noticeable. Where
there had been snow and frozen earth to the
North, the low land was verdant. The only

activity I had seen among the northerners was the grazing of a few emaciated goats; but here the land was fertile and farmers could be seen all over the landscape, tilling the soil. As we approached the floor of the valley, we came upon a highway, level terrain, a warm breeze -- the like of which I hadn't known for a long time. We hurried on to the village of Zacharo.

Shortly after our arrival, the British officer who was in charge of the activity explained that it would be at least a fortnight before the big event would come off. He advised us to make ourselves as comfortable as we could. He promptly issued a shoe box full of Greek Draxmai to each of us for pocket money. I had several million Draxmai.

In the village there were twenty-odd men who had lived in the States for varying periods of time. We talked much of the good things in the USA, but their main topic was, "When can we expect an invasion?"

We tarried a day in that pleasant village, and as suddenly as we'd come, we left. It was decided that for the safety of all, it would be better if we were to move further inland and away from the point of evacuation. Zacharo is on a rail line and was subject to sudden and unexpected visits by the German troops, who were famous for their lack of hospitality. They were present in great numbers at Pyrgos, only a few miles to the north. We retraced our steps to the village of Arini, which nestled at the foot of the mountains, about half way between the summit and Zacharo.

There was much conversation but little activity at Arini. We enjoyed practically every known convenience, except a bath. The food was substantial, though monotonous. We ate goat meat until we began to bleat. We were full of hope. The departure date was set for "tomorrow night" a dozen or more times. Meanwhile, we sat and waited.

During our unhappy stay, I learned a new game. Several partisan soldiers had been detailed as our guards and protectors. They were an irresponsible lot, and, as protectors, they were a liability. There was a goodly supply of the national refresher, ouzo, to be had, and each evening the would-be guards congregated, uninvited, in the home of a villager. After the jug had made a given number of turns around the party, the partisans seemed to decide unanimously and at the same instant that it was time to play a game. By some means that I never completely understood, they would select some member of the group to be "it." The game amounted to something like "hide-and-seek," except the person who was "it" hid and was sought out by the others. Everyone was armed with a machine gun. Whenever the time came to play a game, the signal that I always missed was given, and a solitary individual would leap to his feet and race blindly through the door. The others would sit idly by the fireside and take one last sip. Then, perhaps thirty seconds after the first man had departed, they would set off into

71

the night in an effort to find the man who was hiding. The game was somewhat like touch-tag, except that instead of chasing after the quarry, they would fire upon him with the tommy guns. Practically every night in Arini was like the Fourth of July; I don't know of any case when the player who was "it" was "tagged," but I do remember having been greatly concerned when the searchers turned their guns in the direction of the house in which I was staying. Each night I would pray that they would use up all their ammunition.

The longer we tarried, the rougher things became. Everyone was suffering from a severe case of "cabin fever." Petty quarrels broke out and everyone's nerves were on edge. Each time we were scheduled to go but didn't, the rash broke out anew. Frequently our leader would become panicky and set us to rushing off through the night. These little jaunts, which sometimes lasted a day or two, were occasions of much confusion. It was a matter of hanging together or individually, though, as we could never be sure. To whis-

per "Hun scare" was to forfeit a night's sleep.
On one such evening, I saw Herbie Myers
thrown into a spin. He was especially sensitive to the talk about sneak raids by the enemy. As a deserter, he realized the seriousness
of being captured. One morning at about
0200 hours when we were racing out of town,
a partisan sentry who was serving as an out-
post called to us to halt, speaking in German.
Herbie's immediate and violent reaction
caused me to be almost as alarmed as he was.

7. Away!

It was generally understood that we were to make our return to Italy by boat. There were many false starts. We would trek down to the beach, a distance of eight or ten miles, in the evening and sit among the sand dunes until an hour or so before dawn, at which time we would drag ourselves back to the village and wait for another false start.

At the last village in which we bedded down, I had the good fortune to stay in the home of a young couple who had a nice little four room bungalow and a six month old daughter. I was the proud possessor of a bed, on which I spent many hours each day recuperating. The host's name was Johnnie. He was flat broke, but he was a great operator. Each evening when heading to the beach party, I would ride Johnnie's horse. Before we'd set out he would sneak me a boiled egg, some salt wrapped in a bit of paper, and a crust of bread, which was just that much more than anyone else had. One night as we were hurrying down to the sea, Johnnie's nag, a sad looking creature indeed, stumbled and did a complete somersault, rolling all the way over me. Later, in an effort to repay Johnnie for his generosity, I gave him a woolen suit of underwear, issue type, which had seen much service.

These nightly vigils became monotonous. Finally, on the night of April 3rd, we decided to make one last try. The British Captain in charge, Peter Tetley, was determined to be rid of us. The grousing he had experienced from the Americans made him determined to see us out of the country. He sent many messages to Allied Headquarters in Italy, begging for transportation. We proceeded to the point of evacuation that night, arriving there at about 2215 hours.

At about half a minute past 2215, a tiny light flashed across the waves from out at sea.

Tetley had a candle set inside a perforated fuel
tin, with a gunnysack spread over the outside.
He removed the sack and signaled to the ship,
and immediately there came back a similar
signal. This was it -- at last. Now was the
time to shout, but nobody made a sound. Tetley had a pair of binoculars equipped with an
infrared device which made it possible to see
quite well at night. He passed the glasses
around. I was amazed at what I saw. The
night was very dark, but with the glasses I
could look down past the beaches, at the gen-
tly swelling waves, and out to a number of
small boats being towed ashore by a motor
launch, then beyond them to an Italian destroyer. The destroyer looked big, beautiful,
and promising. Then someone snatched the
glasses from my hands.

As the boats neared the shore, the lines
were cast off from the launch and sailors in
each boat rowed ashore, where the bottoms
grated against the sandy beach. Everyone
raced down to the shore. A few people gathered around each boat and formed a line to

assist in unloading the cargoes of arms and ammunition. There were many partisans present to take charge of these bundles from Britain. As soon as the boats were unloaded, no time was lost reloading them. We scrambled aboard.

Apparently too many chose to ride in the boat into which I had climbed, as it began to ship water. It was necessary for several of us to transship to the motor launch. The destroyer was about a half mile off shore. It didn't seem to take long for us to reach it. The boats drew up at the fantail and we immediately began to climb aboard.

Once aboard we hurried below decks. After a very brief wait, the motors began to turn up and we set off to the north and west. That was just a short while after midnight, in the early morning hours of 4 April 1944. It had been 84 days since we came to Greece.

At about 1700 hours the same day, we dropped the hook at Taranto, Italy. I remember being very pleased about the whole thing.

Epilogue

Following his rescue, Raley was commissioned as a 2nd Lieutenant. He wrote to the families of his perished crew members and began a correspondence with the widow of Lt. Henry Sudol, the copilot of his plane. In February 1947, he visited Mrs. Sudol, the former Lorraine Lineberry, at her home in North Carolina, and married her that July. Raley retired as a Lieutenant Colonel after thirty years in the military and completed another fifteen years in civil service, serving his country a total of forty-five years. He lived his final years with his wife in Winter Springs, Florida, where his friend Neil Daley visited them about once a year.

NAMES OF MY FELLOW CREWMEN:

Capt Robert W. Goen (Millsap, TX)
Pilot

Lt Henry J. Sudol (Passaic, NJ)
Co-Pilot

Lt Bruce E. Hicks (Dodge City, KS)
Navigator

Lt Robert B. Fassett (LaGrange, IL)
Bombardier

TSgt Lucius A. Pittoni (Long Beach, NY)
Radio Operator

SSgt John A. Kemmler (Springfield, IL)
Engineer

SSgt Leonard E. Matkey (Stevens Point, WI)
Ball Turret Gunner

SSgt Eldon C. Steerman (Salina, KS)
Gunner

SIXTEEN B-17 CREWMEN SURVIVED
EVADED CAPTURE, AND ESCAPED TOGETHER

Don Bennett (Alma, NE)

Walter Burry (Minneapolis, MN)

Neil Daley (Bronx, NY)

Thomas Hoffman (Houston, TX)

Leonard Killebrew (Austin, TX)

Jack Murray (New York, NY)

Monte Ogens (Chicago, IL)

Bernard Raftery (Providence, RI)

James A. Raley (Henderson, KY)

Foster Rappele (Pocatello, ID)

Sidney Sherris (Rochester, NY)

Sam Shursky (New York, NY)

Aaron Siegal (New York, NY)

Vern Trinowski (Richland, IN)

Eldon Wallace (Clarksburg, WV)

Tom Woods (New York, NY)

FUNERAL ORATION
FOR THE US AIRMEN WHO DIED
11 JANUARY 1944

Brave and Immortal Dead

In the ancient years the King of Lydia, Krisus, asked Salon the Athenian if he knew a happy man. Salon answered that he knew Tellus the Athenian, who fell fighting heroically for his country and was buried with great ceremony.

But you, IMMORTAL DEAD, are happier than Tellus the Athenian because you fell on these mountains fighting not only for your country, but for the liberation of our country, Greece, and the Universal Liberty.

Alive you came here to our country. Now we say farewell to you, to your new home. Slaves, under the worst slavery, we received you. Now we are free and say goodbye to you from our Land.

All the Greek people together with us, with tears in their eyes, accompany you to your glorious country, our Friend and Ally and Sister Nation, the United States.

God bless your souls, you brave and immortal dead.

~ Bishop of Lambia

Biography

James Andrew Raley

was born in 1916 in Henderson, Kentucky, the eighth of nine children, six of whom survived. He grew up a farm boy, rode horses as effortlessly as walking, wrestled with his brothers, shot rifles, and learned the three "R's" in a one room Catholic school.

Raley left the farm life behind in 1935 to join the Army and serve in Operation Torch, the amphibious invasion of North Africa. In 1943, determined to fulfill his childhood dream of flying, Raley transferred to the Army Air Forces as a tail gunner in the 301st Bombardment Group (Heavy), never imagining how profoundly his life -- and the lives of many others -- would change, as he departed on the morning of his 13th mission.

Made in the USA
Middletown, DE
10 September 2023

38282919R00056